MW01275398

Ravens' Haiku

A collection of haiku
by
Raven Song Community Health Centre
Clinicians

Kelvin Bei
Nico Eichhorst
Eliza Henshaw
Vicki Klassen
Moira Latimer
Jennifer Beaveridge
Cole Stanley
Cherlyn Cortes
Verity Buskard
Michael Fitzmaurice
Michael Burns

Edited and cover art by Kelvin Bei

Contents

Eliza

Must be a bit tired.
Wore my slippers to work, ha!
I really did that.

Hanging at the pool
With the moms; we're spacing out.
Glad I'm not in it.

Ikea montage
Moving in, first house, baby one then two Down size.

12 hours straight at Raven Song
My brain is actually dead now.
Aw.

Anne Murray,
Craigdaroch castle,
Preschool,
Inchworms,
Superman mobile.

In the suburbs
People talk more slowly
And with less passion.
Hmmm. Why?

I have the healthiest liver in the clinic Three point three, yahoo!

Cougar in deep cove
Big cat, out at 6
Grey moon does not seem concerned.

I remember
When that one came in
Now tooth falls out, that baby gone.

What should we do with the farm?
My grandfather is in the buzzing bees.

A secret sister.
For my second half of life...
Coiling DNA.

It's been a long time running
Well worth the wait
Windows down, hand out to the sky.

Looked at facebook feed,
Wow, they are all living large!
Back to real life now.

Bear attack
Bloody water slipping out of neck hole
Survival slim.

Gallop down the street
Find the way yourselves, my girls
Lips closed, I make space.

At around 4ish
It takes more time to say less
Plink plonk type type chart

Vicki

Wearing big earrings
They look silver but not real
Need to buy new ones

I'm so cold today
Rain and noise all around me
Looking for some sun!

Go away, my child
Seems I have too little time
When can I drink wine

Where will my home be?
I love the mountains and beach
I hope I can stay

This is no rabbit
I'm a lion not encaged
Watch out, I will bite!

Out for a run soon
Hope to catch up to that dude
He is cute and fast!

My hair is curly
His face is hairy and big
It is so itchy!

Self care? What is that?
Wine and cheese galore
Hoping for low score

A room with a view
George can grab me anytime
The eternal what?

Sometimes I forget
How fabulous I can be
Remind me again

Fatigue and mucous
Nothing deep and romantic
Makeup and caffeine

Bright dresses and shoes
Not high maintenance, really
I cut my own hair

Wine, cheese, goodnight moon
My son will soon be faster
Mom's day - everyday!

Curly and shiny
Are we closed but not closer?
Moment, can't do it

Bristle, curls and boots
Cold, wet noses in my ears
Time is marching fast

Nico

Kiss me, and again
And again, until we're bronze
Until time finds us

Morning dew
        Blades of grass
        Fields of tears
From the night
        That longs
        For your light

My love, Chimera
Who pulled me in with letters
Pushed away with words

Your marks on my skin
Are fading
I would wear you
Even as a scar

Warm sun
Fragrant flowers
Lazy days
Between the screams
Of butterflies

Snowfall
Covers the world
Beautiful as the desert
And drops of blood

Sea salt on my face
Nurtured, on the knee of god
I ebb in the swell

I dissolve
Into colours
And light
To Break
     Upon
    Your
       Distant
          Shores

Abracadabra
Watch the darkness disappear
Into moon shadows

Spring is in the air
My happiness grows like grass
Time to mow the lawn

Silence unforeseen
Then thought erupt, sinister
Flow along my skin

Each day I'm closer
To the sun and moon and you
And circles of time

I lay beside you
As my fingers trace a path
Through time on your skin

As soft as moon light
As smooth as water worn stone
That lies before me

Red sky this morning
Slip the moorings, back to sea
Far from breaking shores

You rose from the stage
In a bathtub dressed in lace
Are you really dead?

Juliet Tango
And the kiss that lies between
The hours of longing

"Blades of grass
Morning dew

Fields of tears
From the night

That longs
For your light"

Was it in this life
That you first entered my dreams
And captured my heart?

There is no escape
From games that murder Jon Snow
Where all men must die

I dreamt that my love
Would disarm you.
I woke to find
Myself disarmed.

I submit to Fall.
Colours change, and skin turns cold.
My heart beats harder.

Sunshine mosaics
Through antique glass.
Shadows cast from orchids hold time.

The pearl that lies before me
Against the currents
That pull me away.

Carving through the door
Loving through your fingertips
To the other side

This vision
In my mind,
Edges blurred,
Forever in the afterglow

Eyes closed, mind open
Reveal yourself in pieces
I will see you whole

Kelvin

Dark dreary morning
Unexpected rainbow breaks
Yes, Epiphany!

Tic toc
Lub dub
Mind racing
Coffee doesn't help
Productive
Must breathe

Supercalifragilisticexpialidocious
Now repeat

Children love them
Adults loathe them
Gum boots
Gortex
Save the day
Puddles

Melodies like fudge
Undulating crescendos
Piano keys steam

Tears are in my throat
My heart is still in diapers
Duct tape can't fix me

Misleading road signs
Wandering in the desert
I am not alone

Street lights still on
Never ending rain
Wipers swish
Just keep on trucking

Pink clusters on brown twigs
Forgotten hope now remembered
Sakura

Blasted hill
Lungs burning
I am so out of shape
Pride gone
Now walking

Ancient arbors
Fuzzy mice blooming
Into magnificent saucers

Slow smooth talker
Post lunch coma
Woke up to wet arm
Saw drool on sleeve

Whoosh
Saucers tossed over green grass
Mountains slowly obscured by cement

Is that
Dirt on my pants
Or sunshine through the window
I cannot tell

Moonlit radiance
Rock splitting determination
Pose
Snap
Exhale

Moonlit radiance
Illuminates the forest
Breath caught by her glance

Lollipops blooming
Red, yellow, stripes, purple
Too bad not edible

Shirt clings to my chest
Trains to and fro
Rushed and hurried
Life passes by

In between stations
Platform ponderings
Ebb and flow
Journey unknown

Baubles of colour
Often overlooked
In Jordan station
I sit.

People mountain
People sea
Heads bowed to phones
The road ahead unseen

The weirdo on the bench
Mong Kok station
4 haikus
Time now to leave

Traffic muffles bird
Song
Through thick cement
Longing to stay
But cannot

Silence echoes
Loud restlessness
Of a yearning heart
Ear plugs don't work

Post supper saunter
Paused
Street corner sunsets
Lilacs' sweet scent
Inhale

Sunshine after rain
Show golden snails on cement
Long journey ahead

Vibrating strings
Stroke, pluck, pizzicato
The violin sings
Heaven

All attempts failures
Breathing becomes difficult
When is rock bottom?

Rain drops on windshield
Blurs life, emotions, and dreams
Pit-pat therapy

Soft supple red earth
Wedging and kneading the soul
Centering stillness

Song of chickadees
Welcomes me into stillness
Of a forest bath

Clouds shift with the wind
Rocks move as waves come ashore
Cicadas calling

Hostess twinkies cakes
Preservatives in a bag
Goes straight to my hips

Autumn fills my nose
Arbors don their golden cloaks
Alas, the sun sets.

HAIDA GWAII series
Strong westerly wins
Playful pause on George Island
Eager to paddle

Calm seas in morning
11 nautical miles
Sore shoulders and back.

Haida summer camp
Beauty at Benjamin point
Waves crash on to shore

Land of green giants
Spruce, cedar, cypress, hemlock
Old eagles keep watch

Heart humbled by waves
Blanket of stars amazes
Old trees share wisdom

Laying in moss carpet
I feel the island breathe
I follow with mine

Blurry vision
How I wish North Vancouver
Street lights were fireflies.

Rain is miserable
But it makes Sitka spruce
Grow a thousand years

Hidden
By the weeping Beech
Whose fingers reach for water
Exhale

What's lucidity?
Dream reality dreaming
Mind open eyes closed.

The longer I reach
The farther the object of
My affection runs

Great expectations
Only produces heartache
Sadness of longing

Television is
Death to creativity
Must stop to make art

Walking in the rain
Does not feel wet
When heart's heavy with
Loneliness

October windstorm
Technicolor dance of leaves
Acorns fall on roof

Old man waiting at
Bus stop with his cane, staring
Down at the pigeons.

Temporal headache
Grumpy and irritable
When will this day end?!

Chorus of water
Is louder than that of
My mind
Wrens hop and sing.

West coast cloud formations
Moves the heart to dance
Away the depression

Rainbows on the road
Cars driven while leaking gas
Sad drinks for salmon

Late November wind
Scurrying of squirrels make
Rustling happiness

Pigeons continue
Living in concrete forests
After man has left

Running on treadmills
In gyms like mice in cages
A least we're happy?

Cole

Last night, Juniper-
José takes Amber's order.
"Show me your ladies!"

Ted and Donald cruise.
I, oh... want no part of this.
Dubya not so bad.

Micronorbury
Djurforceps delivery
Kelvin baby born

Down in Florida
Old white people everywhere.
Anne Murray's snowbirds?

Just don't let him by!
Two more minutes, for "tripping"
Why can't I score goals?

Chase euphoria
Reality slips away
Methamphetamine

Watch out for Zika!
Flavivirus in the news
Hep C not sexy

>> Wind warning issued >>
       ~ Poppin's umbrella commute ~
                      ...do not overshoot.

Verity

Painted face man
There goes Ziggy Stardust
A space oddity

Check this blank slate
No skull or crossed bones on these arms So much skin to paint

Time change slowed brain
Just one more hour please
Then I'll be ready

Wriggle on, wade out,
Dive under, crash over,
Paddle hard, surf's up!

Blown apart by time
The ephemeral blossom
Crushed underfoot

Rhythm, rate, and pulse
The door open to the flow
Cup to mouth, repeat

Michael F

Funny smell in room
Nico focused super hard
It's smoke from his brain

Jennifer

Wine wine wine
Calling my name
Whistler snow
Addictions and scarves
Vodka

Easter eggs, whip cream,
Colour everywhere
Sunshine, smiles
Ocean breeze

Forty one
Forty one
Forty one
Happy and content
No grey
Wine

Tired. Giggles. Food on floor.
Straw cup leaks. Painting with milk.
Wine

Thoughts
Decisions
Happiness and content
Toddler always hits head
Wine

Sunshine
Noses
Giggles
Smell of lavender at the door
Gin
Wine

Shoes
Floral confidence style
Mountains
Deep breath
Wine

Tea scones toddler smiles
Long plane ride lessons learned
Wine

Busy brain
Fall colours
Smell of rain on warm cement
Wine

Winter
Sparkling lights
Excitement of a toddler
Priceless
Wine

Moira

Go out in the world
Know that if you get lost
I will find you
Always

Monday morning
Play is over, work now
Play at work?
Coffee helps lots

Rain life
Sun heal
Forest breathe
Ocean alive
Seal sweet smooth dog-like, Hi

Must start singing again
Life is so much better with music
Isn't it?

Birdsong greets the dawn
Clear, crisp, new, stunning, perfect
Mocking my regret

Bad news violence
Noise to my mind
Gratitude heals
Simple life
Joy Love

Days in nature
Hardships melt away
Renew
Faith in the world restored!

My Dad says sun and swimming outside
Cure what ails you
I think it's true

Slipping and sliding
Drifting and running
Shoulder season
What to wear?

Coldness creeping in
Beautiful colors
Bears are filling up
Watch out

Raging wind
Torrents of rain
Nature's fury
Only the strong survive

BOO!
I like scaring people
And not just on Halloween
Is that wrong?

Dreams don't lie
They're expressions
Of the soul
Trying to be seen and heard

Sleep dreams can lie
The dreams you have for yourself
And your life
Are your soul

Cherlyn

Back on the Eastside
Hipster bars and coffee shops
Heart and soul remains

ANZA club Friday
Man, can Leslie Logan dance!
Way past my bedtime

On the Sunshine Coast
Our Blue Heeler hikes and swims
A late summer's dream

A Canadian
Feeling election depressed
Trying to find hope

Michael B

Snowy Streets leaden sky
Rain Falls like
Tear drops
Goodbye Mr Winter